The Majesty of Savannah

The Majesty of
SAVANNAH

Photography and Text by
Peter Beney

PELICAN PUBLISHING COMPANY
GRETNA 2001

First printing, 1992
Second printing, 1997
Third printing, 2001

Library of Congress Cataloging-in-Publication Data

Beney, Peter.
    The majesty of Savannah / Peter Beney ; foreword by John Duncan.
       p.   cm.
    ISBN 0-88289-906-6
    1. Savannah (Ga.)—Pictorial works. 2. Dwellings—
Georgia—Savannah—Pictorial works. 3. Interior decoration—
Georgia—Savannah—Pictorial works. I. Title.
F294.S2B46 1992
975.8'724—dc20   92-10968
                                                  CIP

Photo on p. 2: The Tybee Island Lighthouse has guarded the mouth of the Savannah River since 1736. The first ninety-foot-high brick tower was built by William Blithman. Destroyed by a storm, another was erected by Thomas Summer in 1842 and lighted in 1848. A third structure was built by John Mulryne in 1773 and that forms the base of the present lighthouse. The museum is open to the public.

Photo on p. 6: The marsh on Tybee Island at sunset.

Photo on p. 8: Fort Pulaski on Cockspur Island was built between 1829 and 1847 to guard river approaches to Savannah at a cost of $1,000,000 for its 25,000,000 bricks. Seized by Confederates in 1861, it was recaptured by the Union on April 10, 1862 after only a thirty-hour bombardment, thanks to a new rifled canon. Fort Pulaski is open daily.

Printed in Hong Kong
Published by Pelican Publishing Company, Inc.
1000 Burmaster Street, Gretna, Louisiana 70053

To Ellen Louise

Acknowledgments

Many smoothed my way and in particular I'd like to thank: Jenny Stacy of the Savannah Area Convention and Visitors Bureau; Mary Ann Smith of the Savannah Downtown Neighborhood Association; Ester Shaver of E. Shaver, Fine Books; Prof. John Duncan, professor of history at Armstrong State College in Savannah; Frank McGuire for his interest, suggestions, and editorial input; Moakler Processing Service of Atlanta for their flawless E6 processing; museum curators, restaurant managers, and especially the owners of these special homes who gave graciously of their time and made many helpful recommendations.

Contents

Foreword

Savannah was not America's first planned city but some town planners have claimed that it is America's best planned city. Visitors have long noted that Savannah is the most European of American towns. Perhaps even more than its architecture, Savannah's squares are her glory. They assure graceful modern urban living by providing comfortable outdoor space for residents, their children, and pets. The town attracts and breeds artists, writers, and lovable eccentrics.

It is ironic that the majestic city of Savannah had the most humble and harsh beginnings of any of the first settlements of the thirteen original colonies. Founding father James Edward Oglethorpe intended the town to be a fresh start for debtors released from English prisons. Early restrictions included the prohibition on rum or "Strong Waters," "Black Slaves or Negroes," lawyers, and "Papists." Blue laws restricted Sunday travel while requiring church attendance. Charity colonists were given fifty acres of land but this could not be divided, mortgaged, rented, or sold. King George II's royal charter prohibited anyone from owning more than five hundred acres and land could be inherited only by male heirs. Life in early Savannah was short, nasty, and harsh.

Oglethorpe's lasting contribution was his famed Savannah plan. In 1733 on the bank of the Savannah River he laid out four modules or wards. In the center were squares to be used for markets or places of refuge during times of crisis. Nowadays the squares are manicured with hundred-year-old magnolia trees, tall palmetto palms, and majestic live oaks dripping with Spanish moss. Savannah's green squares are Savannah's lungs. Bull Street squares boast the most impressive monuments. Johnson Square has the 1825 Greco-Egyptian obelisk to Quaker Revolutionary War general Nathanael Greene. Wright Square is the site of the Renaissance-style monument to Central of Georgia Railroad founder William Washington Gordon. Chippewa Square is home to Daniel Chester French's 1910 statue of James Edward Oglethorpe. The dramatic 1888 monument to Revolutionary War hero Sgt. William Jasper towers above Madison Square. Monterey Square has the 1855 monument of Count Casimir Pulaski, mortally wounded during the Franco-American attack on British-held Savannah on October 9, 1779.

To the east and west of the squares are public or trust lots and in the older parts of town they still retain their public character, housing courthouses, banks, and churches. To the north and south of the squares are the tithing lots—private homesites originally sixty by ninety feet. Many have since been divided into eastern and western halves. Oglethorpe surrounded the town with a common which allowed the creation of an additional twenty wards and the large Forsyth Park, which contains Savannah's most impressive fountain, the Confederate Monument, two mock forts, and the Spanish-American War monument.

In many ways Savannah's watershed year was 1793, when Yale graduate Eli Whitney invented his famous cotton gin at Caty Greene's Mulberry Grove Plantation just up the Savannah River. Cotton became king and Savannahians began to reap princely incomes. In 1886, architect William G. Preston erected his brick and terra-cotta Savannah Cotton Exchange. Built during the last years of King Cotton, this building was the first in Savannah to be built over air rights. In a sense it is the symbol for Savannah. In front of this building is a handsome mythological griffin fountain.

The town plan of Savannah is eighteenth century, but Savannah's architecture is nineteenth century. Pre-King Cotton buildings in Savannah are few and generally unimpressive. A few builders continued to use the old Georgian or Federal style, but it was English Regency architect William Jay who introduced magnificence into the city. Most of his buildings are now gone, but three Jay houses are owned by the Telfair Academy. Best preserved is the Richardson-Owens-Thomas House Museum on Oglethorpe Square. Underneath the portico is an underground ice well which proves the adage that if you are rich enough, you can live well, any place, any time.

Jay's second survivor is the old Telfair mansion on Barnard Street. By the 1875 will of Miss Mary Telfair her home was to be transformed into the Telfair Academy of Arts and Sciences with the stipulation that the name Telfair be "in larger letters" and occupy "a separate line."

Jay's third masterpiece was the 1819 house for William Scarbrough, the chief backer of the steamship *Savannah*, the first steamship to cross the Atlantic Ocean. The building survived years of hard use as a public school. More recently it was restored by the Historic Savannah Foundation and since 1990 it has come under the ownership of the Telfair.

In the Jay style is the 1820 Wayne Gordon House Museum, affectionately known to many locals as "the birthplace" and which one outsider said he was astounded to learn is not in Bethlehem but at the corner of Bull and Oglethorpe Avenue in Savannah, Georgia.

In the 1840s and 1850s the Greek Revival style was the fashion. Notable examples are Christ Episcopal Church on Johnson Square, built by James Hamilton Couper in 1838, and the U.S. Custom House on Bay Street, built by John S. Norris in 1848-52. The outstanding example of Greek Revival domestic architecture is the Champion-McAlpin House on Orleans Square. In the 1930s novelist Harry Hervey used it as his setting for *The Damned Don't Cry*, and in recent years it has become the headquarters for the Georgia State Society of the Cincinnati.

John Norris also built a Gothic home for English cotton factor Charles Green on Madison Square in 1853. This house served as General Sherman's headquarters during his 1864-65 stay in Savannah. Since 1942 it has served as the parish house and rectory for St. John's Episcopal Church. Norris also built the Italianate house for cotton factor Andrew Low on Lafayette Square in 1849 and since 1928 it has been the headquarters for the Georgia chapter of Colonial Dames of America.

After the Civil War William G. Preston used the Romanesque style for the 1889 old Chatham County Court House on Wright Square. A Savannah wit once called this the hatch, match, and dispatch office, because birth, marriage, and death records were kept there. Preston repeated the style in his 1893 Savannah Volunteer Guards Armory on Madison Square, now the centerpiece building for the Savannah College of Art and Design.

Second Empire Baroque was Savannah's most urban, exuberant, and sculptural building style; witness the 1873 Hamilton-Turner House on Lafayette Square and the Thomas-Levy House on Monterey Square.

The 1850 observations on Savannah by Swedish feminist Fredrika Bremer remain valid today. To her, Savannah was "the most charming of cities" and "an assemblage of villas which have come together for company." Time has mellowed this old town. Major fires occurred in 1796 and 1820. There have been numerous hurricanes and a frightening earthquake in 1886. Worst of all Savannah has experienced the indignity of two military occupations, by the British in 1778-82 and Federal troops in 1864-65.

To the fast-paced outsider the town might be a place of live oaks and dead people, but here the past is not past. It is very much alive. The town cemeteries are frequented by natives and tourists. Colonial Park Cemetery is the oldest and the resting place for Button Gwinnett, one of the three Georgia signers of the Declaration of Independence, and also for Gen. Lachlan McIntosh, who killed him in a 1777 duel. Visitors are challenged to find the oldest gravestone, which dates from 1762. The old Jewish Cemetery and the Sheftall family cemetery are on the west side of town and farther out is Laurel Grove. The most romantic is Bonaventure Cemetery, on the Wilmington River. Buried here are Savannah's most prominent man of letters, Conrad Aiken, and the lyricist Johnny Mercer. In the spring Bonaventure azaleas are so spectacular that some venture the belief that to be buried there is almost as good as being alive anywhere else.

Savannah at times is the haughty aristocrat with its exclusive Oglethorpe Club and debutante parties; it is often obsessed with its own lineage. Others are amused by its provinciality and point out that this is a town founded on a bluff and its main street is Bull. Like Charlestonians in South Carolina and the Chinese, Savannahians are noted for eating lots of rice, worshipping their ancestors, and speaking a foreign dialect. In the South Carolina Low Country it is called Gullah and in Georgia it is called Geechee. It is a unique coastal blend of English, African, and West Indian accents and inflections.

Few debtors actually came to Georgia and the English worthy poor became the basic stock for the colony. The famous John Wesley came to Savannah in 1736 to minister to the Indians, but he ended up as rector of the Anglican (now Episcopal) Christ Church. His successor was George Whitefield, notable for his 1740 founding of Bethesda Orphanage, which claims to be America's oldest orphanage.

In July of 1733 Sephardic Jews came fleeing the Portuguese Inquisition. They established Mickve Israel congregation, the third oldest Jewish congregation in the country. Their Torah is the oldest one in the nation, and the 1876 temple on Monterey Square is the only U.S. synagogue to use the Gothic style of architecture.

Oglethorpe brought in a regiment of Scottish Highlanders and in 1755, Savannah's Independent Presbyterian Congregation was established. Since 1819 the congregation has worshipped at the elegant Sir Christopher Wren style church at Bull and Oglethorpe Avenue. Ellen Axson Wilson was the granddaughter of the minister and has the distinction of being the only First Lady from Savannah.

In 1734 came Lutherans banished by order of the Catholic archbishop of Salzburg. Most who came to Georgia settled in the separate community of Ebenezer, in adjoining Effingham County. By 1741 Savannah Lutherans had established their congregation, now known as the Lutheran Church of the Ascension on Wright Square.

Savannah Baptists were granted property in Washington Square in 1791. This was exchanged for property on Franklin Square in 1795 and since 1833, they have worshipped in Chippewa Square. Negro slavery was allowed in 1751, and the First African Baptist Church, on Franklin Square, and Bryan Baptist Church, on Bryan Street, claim descent from the nation's first black Baptist Congregation of 1788.

Roman Catholics too were eventually tolerated and the Cathedral of St. John the Baptist, on Abercorn Street, was erected in 1876. Savannah's St. Patrick's Day Parade is one of the largest in the world. Beer and grits are often colored green and attempts have actually been made to dye the Savannah River.

Unitarians, it is said, profess a trinity of beliefs: the unity of God, the brotherhood of man, and the vicinity of Boston. Savannah Unitarians are proud of James Pierpoint, who composed and copyrighted his famous "Jingle Bells" while serving as organist for the Savannah congregation in the 1850s.

Methodists justly claim the oldest pristine church building in Savannah— Trinity Methodist Church, the work of John B. Hogg in 1848. Wesley Methodist Church, on Calhoun Square, was built in 1876-90 as a memorial to John and Charles Wesley with contributions from Methodists all over the world.

Over the years others have come to the city including Greeks and Chinese. More recently Cubans, Vietnamese, and Mexicans have arrived to call it home. All have added to the fabric of Savannah's coat of many colors and this ethnic diversity is one of its greatest assets. Natives love their birthplace, tourists are welcomed, and newcomers even more so. Savannah loves anyone who loves Savannah.

JOHN DUNCAN

The Majesty of Savannah

Museum Houses

Richardson-Owens-Thomas House

124 Abercorn Street—
Oglethorpe Square

The parterre garden and carriage house. The garden dates from the 1950s restoration.

Richard Richardson, a wealthy cotton trader, in 1816 gave the twenty-five-year-old English architect William Jay (1792-1837) his first commission in Savannah. Jay, who was to leave a distinguished mark on the city, arrived in 1817 and supervised construction of this Regency masterpiece.

Richardson lost his home to creditors in the 1820s and in 1830 it was purchased by a prominent Savannahian named George Owens. It remained in the Owens family until 1951, when George's granddaughter, Miss Margaret Thomas, willed it to the Telfair Academy of Arts and Sciences. Today it is a National Historic Landmark Museum where visitors can appreciate the genius of William Jay's design.

Richardson-Owens-Thomas House, west elevation, was completed in 1819.

This classic Regency balcony with cast-iron grillwork is where the Marquis de Lafayette reviewed troops marching past on the occasion of the fiftieth anniversary of the Declaration of Independence in 1825.

The entrance hall, with its bust of Lord Byron, features Greek columns with gilt capitals and stairs inlaid with brass.

The dining room continues the Greek key design motif over the alcove; doors are curved to fit the shape of the room; the chandelier is French tole (painted tin), gold on copper, ca. 1800. The attractive table and chairs were crafted by Henry Connely of Philadelphia in 1820.

The music room boasts a harp from St. Petersburg, Russia, ca. 1830, Rosewood English chairs, ca. 1820, and a Duncan Phyfe sofa, ca. 1810.

Note the Grecian couch of horsehair and an English gaming table, ca. 1820.

The drawing room with a settee by Duncan Phyfe, ca. 1800, and a marble mantel with sculpture of a Greek woman with an eagle. The unusual ceiling has fan-shaped moldings in gold leaf.

The secretary/bookcase is from New York, ca, 1805.

Splendid antiques in the bedroom testify that this house is one of the gems of Savannah.

Scarbrough House

41 Martin Luther King, Jr., Blvd.

Savannah cotton factor William Scarbrough, the primary investor in the record-breaking SS *Savannah*, had this English Regency mansion built in time for Pres. James Monroe's visit in 1819. Monroe's stay there, the classical splendor of William Jay's design, and its elegant furnishings made the Scarbrough House the center of Savannah's social life. In later years numerous alterations were made, as the house served as a public school from 1878 to 1972. Then restoration began, and in 1977, Scarbrough House opened as a museum and the headquarters of the Historic Savannah Foundation. Designated a National Historic Landmark, Scarbrough House stands as one of William Jay's finest creations. Since 1990 the house has been owned by the Telfair Academy.

Scarbrough House, east elevation, was designed by William Jay and completed in May 1819.

The oak reception room is octagonal, with an English marble mantel, ca. 1810, original oil-burning English chandeliers, and English celestial and terrestrial globes made by J. & W. Cary, ca. 1800.

Telfair Academy

121 Barnard Street

William Jay designed and built this mansion in 1819 for Alexander Telfair (1792-1832), a prominent Savannahian and son of a former Georgia governor, Edward Telfair (1743-1807). His daughter, Mary Telfair (1789-1875), bequeathed the house to the Georgia Historical Society in 1875. The Telfair Academy of Arts and Sciences opened in 1886, after remodelling directed by New York architect Detlef Lienau, as the Southeast's first public art museum.

Telfair Academy, east elevation, is a superb example of English Regency architecture.

The dining room, with a reproduction of a nineteenth-century Brussels carpet, has a block-printed panoramic mural called Les Monument de Paris, a pair of carved mahogany and caned Grecian couches by Duncan Phyfe, ca. 1820, and a classic mahogany sideboard by the same cabinetmaker, ca. 1825. Visitors to this spectacular room are left with lasting memories.

The double parlor, northeast, with a painting of Alexander Telfair above the Frazee mantel; also the desk belonged to Margaret Telfair.

Telfair Academy's double parlor, southeast, has a marble mantel carved by John Frazee and a painting of James Habersham hanging above.

The hallway has a skylight roof and plaster casts of the Elgin Marbles, part of major remodelling in the 1880s by Detlef Lienau.

The Telfair Academy exhibition hall has impressive iron columns at its entrance.

James Moore Wayne House
Birthplace of Juliette Gordon Low
142 Bull Street

This English Regency mansion just south of Wright Square was built in 1820, architect unknown, for James Moore Wayne, serving at the time as Savannah's mayor. William Gordon acquired the house in 1831 and his son, father of Juliette Gordon Low, later inherited it. In 1886 he hired architect Detlef Lienau to enlarge the house, adding an attic and a side piazza. The Gordon family retained the house until 1953, when the Girl Scouts of the U.S.A. bought and restored it as a memorial to their founder, Juliette Gordon Low.

James Moore Wayne House, east elevation. The parterre garden was restored in 1950.

Juliette Gordon Low, born on Halloween in 1860, was a remarkable person who never let her deafness prevent her from exploring her talents to their fullest—painting, sculpting, writing plays, and performing in them. She travelled widely with her husband, William MacKay Low, but it was an unhappy marriage. Juliette spent time in England after William's death in 1905, and while there in 1911, she met Robert Baden-Powell, founder of the Boy Scouts and Girl Guides. The next year Juliette returned to Savannah and in March organized the first Girl Guide troop with eighteen girls. Changing the name to

The back parlor or family room has an exceptional portrait of Juliette Low by Jonnieaux of Belgium, ca. 1922. These rooms can be divided by heavy wooden sliding doors flanked by Ionic columns.

Girl Scouts in 1913, the organization grew rapidly into a national movement which today has over three million members.

Juliette Gordon Low taught girls not to narrow their horizons, but to pursue any profession that interested them. She encouraged active citizenship. Girl Scouts of the U.S.A. maintains her birthplace as a repository of 6,000 artifacts pertaining to life in the nineteenth century. The house is a National Historic Landmark, and as a Girl Scout Center receives visitors from all over the world.

The replica of a portrait of Juliette Gordon Low hanging in the library was painted in 1887 by Edward Hughes.

The dining room of the house has a distinctive Turkish chandelier and a portrait of Juliette Low's mother, Eleanor Kinzie Gordon, painted by Alice Shurleff in 1905.

Here is General and Mrs. Gordon's bedroom, with the family crib and Juliette Gordon's birth bed.

Grandmother Gordon's bedroom is furnished with her original four-poster bed and a quilt that she made.

Isaiah Davenport House

324 East State Street

Isaiah Davenport arrived in Savannah from Rhode Island in 1799 at the age of fifteen and soon established himself as a successful builder. In 1818 he was elected alderman and began his splendid two-story brick home facing Columbia Square. Davenport was a renowned carpenter and his classical detailing makes this house ideally representative of American Federal architecture.

Proposed demolition of the Davenport House in 1955 served as the catalyst for Savannah residents to undertake their restoration efforts in concert under the aegis of the Historic Savannah Foundation founded that year. From then on Savannah's preservation movement bloomed, culminating in 1966 when Oglethorpe's planned city of squares and wards was designated a National Historic Landmark.

The Isaiah Davenport House, south elevation, on Columbia Square was built in 1820.

The Davenport House has Tuscan columns that frame the main stairway, creating a dramatic entrance.

View up the stairwell spiraling up to the third floor of the Davenport House.

The magnificent entrance hall of Davenport House, looking toward Columbia Square. The tall clock was made by John Bell for Mr. Nathan Reed of Savannah.

The Davenport House grand parlor is breathtaking with Ionic Tuscan columns and arches. Over the original marble mantelpiece hangs a portrait of Mrs. Brailsford painted by Jeremiah Theus of South Carolina in 1750. The matching chair and settee are Hepplewhite and the sofa is Empire, ca. 1820.

This magnificent dining room is off the main hallway. The portrait is of Gen. Charles Williams, the chairs are Chippendale, and the table is Hepplewhite. The dining set on display is by Davenport of Stoke-on-Trent, England, ca. 1810-20.

The main bedroom of the Davenport House has a canopied Sheraton reeded four-poster bed from 1790 and a Jacobean tallboy from 1820.

The master bedroom with an antique cradle and a christening gown laid out on the 1810 Southern canopy bed.

Andrew Low House

329 Abercorn Street

This imposing villa was built in the Italianate style by New York architect John S. Norris (1804-76) for merchant Andrew Low in 1849. No expense was spared. His son William inherited the house in 1886, months before marrying Juliette Gordon. Detlef Lienau supervised some remodelling at that time, installing a second-floor bathroom.

Detailed cast-iron railings embellish the south wall.

After William Low died in 1905, Juliette Gordon Low lived alone in this house, founding the Girl Scouts of the U.S.A. in the reception room in 1912. Upon her death here in 1927, the National Society of Colonial Dames in Georgia bought the estate as its headquarters and they continue to guide its restoration and maintenance.

Andrew Low House, east elevation, faces Lafayette Square.

This front reception room is where Juliette Gordon Low convened the first meeting of the Girl Scouts of the U.S.A.

The egg and dart plasterwork in the entrance hallway is in a passionflower design; note the Regency Girondole looking glass, ca. 1820, and the sofa by Duncan Phyfe, ca. 1820.

The pianoforte in the reception room is by H & W Geib, New York, ca. 1820.

The pianoforte in the front parlor is by John Broadwood & Son, London, ca. 1810.

The magnificent double-bevel Regency mirror, ca. 1886, dominates the front parlor; the Wilton loom carpet from England dates from 1810 and the matching Meridian couch, chair, and stool from 1845.

The Andrew Low House back parlor, looking toward the front, features a chandelier from Bristol, England, ca. 1790, a brass cathedral lamp in foreground, ca. 1840, and drapes by Scalamandre, ca. 1810.

The back parlor of the Andrew Low House displays a book press and an 1852 edition of a Shakespeare elephant folio reader, illustrated by Boydell, that is opened here for a rare inspection.

The dining room was comfortably furnished by the Colonial Dames with a Sheraton sideboard, Duncan Phyfe Regency table and chairs, Crown Derby china, and carpet and drapes by Scalamandre.

Andrew Low House's principal bedroom, called the "Atlanta Room," is furnished in a classical 1840s style. The Duncan Phyfe four-poster bed is from 1815. Argand lamps are on the mantel with an Eli Terry clock, ca. 1810.

The east bedroom offers a wonderful view out the window onto Lafayette Square, and this desk was used by English novelist William Makepeace Thackeray when he was a houseguest in 1853 and 1856. Andrew Low hosted Robert E. Lee in 1870.

A close-up of the Duncan Phyfe wardrobe in the Atlanta bedroom.

These dolls in the "Augusta" children's room of the Andrew Low House are over one hundred years old.

Green-Meldrim House
Parish House of St. John's
Episcopal Church

14 West Macon Street—
Madison Square

John S. Norris in 1853 built the grandest house in Savannah at the time for shipowner and cotton merchant Charles Green at a cost of $93,000. Many architectural critics consider it the best example of a Gothic Revival house in the South. At Green's invitation, General Sherman made it his headquarters when Union troops occupied Savannah in December 1864, staying more than two months. From here Sherman sent his famous Christmas wire to President Lincoln, delivering the city as a holiday gift. Upon Green's death in 1881 the house was inherited by his son Edward. However, financial difficulties compelled Edward to sell in 1892 to Judge Peter Meldrim. In 1943 this distinguished family sold the mansion to St. John's Episcopal Church and since then it has served as the parish and rectory. In 1976 it was designated a National Historic Landmark.

Green-Meldrim House, second floor, south bay. The heart-of-pine floors are original.

Ornate cast-iron porches and fences are a distinctive feature of the Green-Meldrim House.

The northeast room has the oldest collection of English furniture in Savannah: a seventeenth-century English table, Windsor chairs with pierced splats, and in the foreground a Gothic sixteenth-century horizontal chest.

The entrance hallway, whose original tile floors were faithfully reproduced during the 1968 renovation; the chandelier is original and the woodwork is in American black walnut.

In the southwest sitting room, the Spanish chest or vargueno between the windows is ca. sixteenth century, and the wing chair beside it is a seventeenth-century "William and Mary."

The north drawing room of the Green-Meldrim House has an American Empire sofa, original gas chandeliers, and a gold-leaf mirror from Austria over the Carrara marble mantel.

The grand south drawing room, looking to the north parlor, shows the original ornate cornices of stucco that are throughout the first floor.

A corner of the south drawing room displays a harp, gold-leaf Austrian mirrors, and a Carrara marble fireplace that has an ash drop to the basement.

The Green-Meldrim House music area in the south drawing room with a Vose piano from Boston, ca. 1860, and overhead a copy of Raphael's painting The Transfiguration, *which was the last painting he did before his death (the original hangs in the Uffizi in Florence).*

34

The southwest bedroom of the Green-Meldrim House was occupied by General Sherman during his stay from December 1864 to February 1865; the four-poster mahogany bed, ca. 1825, has carved rope footposts.

In the second-floor hall there is a classic Victorian wall clock, and a painting of the waterfront by Savannah artist Myrtle Jones King over an American Empire sofa.

The Meldrim Memorial Library has portraits over the mantel of (left to right): Judge Peter Meldrim, Bishop Stephen Elliott—first rector of St. John's, and Frances Casey Meldrim.

St. John's Episcopal Church

*1 West Macon Street—
Madison Square*

*The exquisite stained-glass windows
come from England.*

*St. John's Episcopal Church was built
in 1852 in the Gothic Revival style.
The church is famous for its chimes.*

The interior of St. John's Episcopal Church.

King-Tisdell Cottage Museum

514 East Huntingdon Street

King-Tisdell Cottage, originally at 516 Ott Street, was built in 1896 by W. W. Aimar, who owned a local planing mill. Eugene Dempsey King bought the house in 1910 and lived there until his death in 1941, after which his widow married Robert Tisdell. Distinguished by elaborate latticework on the porch and dormers, the cottage was moved in 1980 to its present location by a consortium of preservationist groups when area

The basement museum of King-Tisdell Cottage showing items representative of the life of coastal blacks.

urban renewal threatened it. Today the King-Tisdell Cottage is operated by the Savannah-Yamacraw Chapter of the Association for the Study of Afro-American Life and History.

The King-Tisdell Cottage Museum is dedicated to preserving the culture of coastal blacks of the 1890s

The parlor has period antiques and portraits of people associated with the house.

The rear garden and "Free to Fly" fountain created in 1990 by Georgia blacksmith Ivan Bailey.

The King-Tisdell Cottage Museum displays letters and documents depicting coastal black history.

Historic District

Oglethorpe Statue in Chippewa Square

James Edward Oglethorpe and 120 colonists arrived at Yamacraw Bluff on the Savannah River on February 12, 1733, after crossing the Atlantic from Gravesend, England.

The statue of General Oglethorpe in Chippewa Square was done by Daniel Chester French in 1910.

A stone bench on West Bay Street marks the site where General Oglethorpe set up his first campsite.

Factor's Walk

Savannah Riverfront along Bay Street

High on the bluff of the Savannah River, Factor's Walk was the eighteenth- and nineteenth-century center of Savannah's commercial life, housing cotton warehouses and offices for traders in cotton, rice, silk, and indigo. At its height more than two million bales of cotton moved through Savannah.

Since 1977 these restored warehouses have welcomed visitors to more than seventy-five museums, restaurants, shops, studios, and taverns, making the area again the center of historic Savannah.

Factor's Walk on Bay Street in the early 1800s teemed with cotton factors or traders, merchant seamen, and dock workers whose efforts made Savannah the Atlantic coast's second busiest port.

Fortunes were made on Factor's Walk.

Cobblestones from the ballast of ships pave ramps and streets.

A nine-block brick concourse invites picnicking, strolling, and dreaming of bygone days.

Savannah Cotton Exchange

100 East Bay Street

Built over Factor's Walk, the Savannah Cotton Exchange of 1886 was designed by Boston architect William Gibbons Preston. It is thought to be the first time in America a building was constructed over an existing street.

Only the invention of the cotton gin in 1793 by Eli Whitney of Connecticut made possible the processing of large amounts of cotton.

Whitney perfected the cotton gin while a guest at General Greene's Mulberry Grove Plantation near Savannah.

By 1820 trading at the Savannah Cotton Exchange set world cotton prices.

Forsyth Park

Bull Street between Gaston Street and Park Avenue

Forsyth Park's twenty acres typify Savannah's open areas, giving the city a country atmosphere. Azaleas blooming in the spring make a spectacular sight.

Forsyth Park's ornate fountain dates from 1858.

Franklin Square is on Montgomery Street between Bryan and Congress streets. It was laid out in 1790 and named for Benjamin Franklin.

Savannah Squares

Savannah's twenty-four residential squares, the heart of Oglethorpe's town plan, give the historic district its distinctive character.

Johnson Square is on Bull Street between Bay and Congress streets, and is where Gen. Nathanael Greene is buried.

Reynolds Square is on Abercorn between Bryan and Congress streets. Georgia Methodists erected Marshall Daugherty's statue of John Wesley in 1969.

Reynolds Square with a profusion of brilliant flowers.

Monterey Square, on Bull Street between Taylor and Gordon streets, features the Casimir Pulaski monument in honor of the Polish nobleman who perished in the Siege of Savannah in 1779.

Lafayette Square on Abercorn Street between Harris and Charlton streets, laid out in 1837, has the Cathedral of St. John the Baptist in the background.

45

Ships of the Sea Museum

503 East River Street

Exhibit room of *Ships of the Sea Museum, with a model of* SS Savannah *on left and sailing ship* Savannah *on right.*

The SS *Savannah*, with auxiliary steam power, sailed from Savannah on May 22, 1819 and reached Liverpool, England, on June 20, making it the first steamship to cross the Atlantic. Local businessman William Scarbrough promoted this enterprise. The SS *Savannah* had a ninety-horsepower engine and boiler, augmenting its paddle wheels, sails, and spars, to propel the ninety-eight-foot-long ship that weighed 350 tons. With timely trade a reality, a new merchantile era was born.

Ships of the Sea Museum has three floors of maritime exhibits overlooking the Savannah River.

46

Pirates' House

20 East Broad at Bay Street

The Pirates' House occupies the area of the Trustees' Garden, America's first public experimental garden. Shortly after his arrival in 1733, General Oglethorpe cultivated a ten-acre plot, modelled after the Chelsea Botanical Garden in London, which he called the Trustees' Garden. He proceeded to plant cotton, fruit trees, hemp, indigo, medicinal herbs, and olives. There were high hopes for mulberry trees for producing silk and grapes for wine, but neither were grown successfully.

The Herb House, adjacent to the Pirates' House, was built in 1734, making it the oldest house in Georgia.

However, this garden proved that cotton and peaches flourished in Savannah's soil and both became mainstays of Georgia agriculture.

The Pirates' House has been an inn ever since 1753.

The Herb House is now one of fifteen rooms for fine dining.

The Captain's Room of the Pirates' House is one of the most popular dining rooms, with its ceiling of hand-hewn beams with wooden pegs.

The Jolly Roger Room has an antique bottle collection and an old organ.

The Pirates' House, overlooking the garden.

The old well in the yard area of the Pirates' House.

A window of the Pirates' House looking out onto East Broad Street.

William Taylor House

206 West Bay Street

This oldest ballast-stone cotton warehouse in the U.S. was built by William Taylor around 1818 and modernized into a private home in 1970 by Savannah architect Juan C. Bertotto.

A massive wheel, made of Georgia pine by Geechee slaves, hoisted cotton bales to the upper levels of the warehouse and is now mounted for display over the main stairway of Taylor House. The balcony sitting area has a round brick fireplace with a copper hood and stack as its centerpiece. The north-facing skylight stretches the length of the room.

Factor's Walk entrance to Taylor House, south elevation. The Bay Street entrance is on the top level. At midlevel, by a wooden bridge walkway, is the Bay Street access to a gallery/studio.

Taylor House, riverfront, north elevation. Now art galleries, this was the main frontage when the building was a cotton warehouse. The original copper roof is the only one left on River Street.

The Taylor House downstairs dining and sitting room supply modern comfort in an historical setting.

Christ Episcopal Church

28 Bull Street

John Wesley was rector of the Anglican (now Christ Episcopal) Church, the first church formed in the Savannah colony. While there Wesley began Sunday School classes, and it may have been the first Protestant Sunday School. He also published the original English hymnal in America.

The splendid interior of Christ Episcopal Church.

Christ Episcopal Church was built in 1838, replacing two earlier buildings.

Eliza Jewett House

326 Bull Street

The Eliza Jewett House personifies the loving care given to restoring Savannah's historic homes. Built in 1834, the house was renovated by Alida Harper Fowlkes in the 1950s, giving early impetus to the Savannah Historic District preservation movement. The present owners finished the restoration in 1975, from the brick-covered-with-stucco exterior facing Madison Square to the quiet elegance of the interior. The stately columns before the main stairway beckon one to enter a world of contemplation, refinement, and good taste.

Eliza Jewett House, west elevation, sits on Madison Square in serene elegance.

The Jewett House has a long entrance hall, typical of Savannah homes, and a dramatic main staircase.

Adjoining parlors are divided by white Ionic columns with pilasters support-ing a central arch. Matching marble fireplaces and period furniture set a mood of contentment in the Jewett House.

The striking rear dining room has a crystal chandelier which is reflected in the gold-leaf framed bevelled mirror over the mantel. Polished pine floors are throughout the ground floor.

The Olde Pink House Restaurant

23 Abercorn Street

James Habersham, Jr., built this Georgian mansion on Reynolds Square in 1771 and lived there thirty-one years. Though educated in England, Habersham was active in the revolutionary movement to free the colonies of British rule. Later he was speaker of the Georgia legislature and a trustee of Franklin College, which became the University of Georgia.

Not long after Habersham's death, the house was acquired by the Bank of the United States. The Planters Bank of Georgia opened in it in 1812 as one of the first registered banks in the state. Then extensive alterations were made to the house to serve its commercial purpose. A new north wing was added, bank vaults installed, and a one-story Greek portico with four Doric columns attached to the front entrance.

The building housed different businesses over the years, coming to be known as the Olde Pink House as the native brick bled through the plaster walls and changed the color to a warm pink.

In 1970 restaurateurs Herschel McCallar and Jeffrey Keith bought and completely restored the Olde Pink House, opening in June 1971 for gourmet dining.

The Olde Pink House Restaurant dominates Reynolds Square.

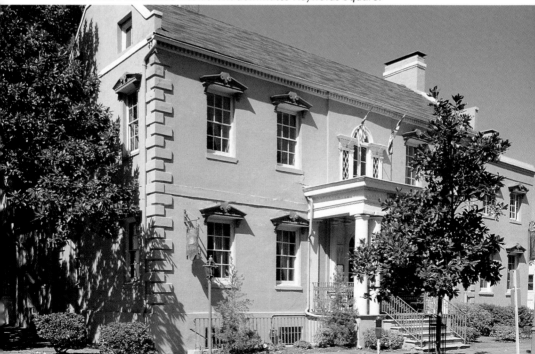

The front dining room of the Olde Pink House Restaurant overlooks Reynolds Square.

The Olde Pink House back dining room has an iron vault door from its days as a bank.

In the Olde Pink House upstairs hall there is a couch that once was used as a bed for coach drivers.

The Olde Pink House Restaurant upstairs parlor.

The Olde Pink House upstairs dining room still has its wrought-iron gate.

Planters Tavern is in the basement of the Olde Pink House and, with two open fireplaces, it is an ideal place to share memories.

Hamilton-Turner House

330 Abercorn Street

The Hamilton-Turner House, a fine example of Second Empire Baroque architecture, was built in 1873 for a former Savannah mayor. At the turn of the century, Savannah social life revolved around this splendid mansion and its popularity never diminished. Today it is open to the public for guided tours.

The Japanese iron ducks on the table are 100 years old.

Hamilton-Turner House, west elevation, on Lafayette Square.

The parlor has a lovely Victorian English tea set.

Note the Belgian crystal chandelier in the front hallway of the Hamilton-Turner House. The hall stand contains a petticoat mirror.

A live parrot occupies the north window of the music room.

This American slant-top desk from the late nineteenth century is popular with visitors.

The Hamilton-Turner House dining room has twenty-four-carat gold-plated Italian candlesticks gracing the table.

This spectacular ceiling-to-floor Empire mahogany four-poster bed with full tester practically fills the bedroom.

American porcelain vases, ca. 1900.

Especially striking are the arched doorways that appear throughout the house.

Colonial Park Cemetery

Abercorn and Oglethorpe Streets

Colonial Park Cemetery, within the Historic District, is the oldest in Savannah, established by early settlers in 1750. Walking through its stillness provides a fascinating glimpse into the past.

A duelist's grave in Colonial Park Cemetery; many colonists met their end defending their honor.

Declaration of Independence signer Button Gwinnett is buried here.

Cathedral of St. John the Baptist

222 East Harris Street

The Parish of St. John the Baptist dates from 1799 and the Victorian Gothic cathedral was erected in 1876. The two spires were added in 1896, the rectory in 1889. Damaged by fire in 1898, the cathedral was rebuilt in 1899 and rededicated one year later. All church windows come from Innsbruck, Austria and murals depicting biblical stories were installed in 1912 under the direction of Savannah artist Christopher Murphy (1869-1939). Structural damage required the cathedral to be closed in 1984 while repairs were made, and the 15,856-square-foot church reopened in 1985.

Cathedral of St. John the Baptist looking from Lafayette Square.

Cathedral of St. John the Baptist seats 1,000 including the balcony.

John J. Powers House

424 Habersham Street

The John J. Powers House was built by a prominent banker of that name on Whitefield Square in 1896.

The John J. Powers House was re-decorated by its present owner in 1987. The entrance hall archway is curtained and the hand-painted wall continues the motif; the polished pine floors are original to this magnificent Victorian house.

The parlor of the John J. Powers House has sliding pocket windows ten feet high for ventilation on long hot summer days.

The dining room features a hand-painted decorative motif and pine furniture.

Magnolia Place Inn

503 Whitaker Street

This Victorian mansion was built in 1878 for J. Guerard Heyward, a descendant of Declaration of Independence signer Thomas Heyward, as Magnolia Hall. Pulitzer Prize winning Savannah poet Conrad Aiken was born here in 1889. Today this popular inn serves up Southern hospitality, with a tradition of afternoon tea, and modern pleasures like jacuzzi baths and a private garden hot tub.

Magnolia Place Inn bedroom fireplace tiles were hand-painted by James Achille de Caradeuc.

The Magnolia Place Inn has unusual green climbing shrubbery growing on its steps and sweeping verandas overlooking Forsyth Park.

The warm parlor has antique English furniture and a hand-painted fireplace.

The beautifully carved wooden fireplace in the bedroom is original to the house. Lavish drapes and bedcovers make this room a favorite.

This bedroom features a four-poster bed with a crochet canopy and a Chinese Nichols Deco Oriental rug. The English faux-bamboo armoire was made from Southern pine in 1870.

The stairwell has a skylight over it with hand-painted clouds in a sky motif; against the wall are silk kimonos in a crane pattern, ca. 1850.

Ballastone Inn

14 East Oglethorpe Avenue

The Ballastone Inn has had as colorful a past as any Savannah landmark. The original land grant dates from 1733 and the property passed through several hands until 1838, when George Anderson built the existing structure. Capt. Henry Blun bought the residence in 1873 and engaged the Boston architect William G. Preston to enlarge it into this Victorian mansion, named for the stones used in its foundation. After 1910 the house served as a boardinghouse, a bordello, and as the York apartments after World War II. In

Ballastone Inn, south and east elevation.

1969 the neighboring Girl Scouts of the U.S.A. saved it from further deterioration by using it for their office space. The Ballastone was sold in 1980 to Tarby Bryant, owner of the Desoto Hotel, who spent $2,000,000 turning it into a modern bed and breakfast inn. In 1988 new owners spent $300,000 more finishing the renovation effort, tastefully adding antiques throughout, reminders of a glorious past.

Ballastone Inn has a charming side garden courtyard where breakfast is served.

The Ballastone Inn has a 175-year-old harp gracing its richly furnished parlor.

The Queen Anne staircase makes the entrance hall special.

The Victoria Suite features antiques from that period. Each room is decorated in a thematic style.

The Ballastone Inn offers a full-service bar with a cozy fireplace.

Stoddard-Lawton House

15 West Perry Street

This property was first given to the Methodist Parsonage by the mayor in 1817, and they apparently built a dwelling as indicated by the 1819 tax digest. In maps of 1853 a small wooden house was marked. John Stoddard, a wealthy planter and merchant, bought the property in 1857, however it is not certain if he built on it. The present house was built in 1867-68 by William Hunter, who spared no expense in its construction. Brig. Gen. Alexander Robert Lawton acquired the house in 1871. Having led a distinguished military career, he was appointed to diplomatic posts abroad. When he

Note the unusually wide front steps leading to impressive hand-carved entrance doors.

returned he retired to the house. After his death it became a rooming house. Then the house lay empty for many years and fell into disrepair, before being restored.

The present owner bought the Stoddard-Lawton House in 1971 and restored it to its former grandeur.

The Stoddard-Lawton House entrance hallway has bold wallpaper. Large doorways leading to the parlor and dining room flank a beautiful antique cabinet clock by M. Walker of Bolton, England.

The bright parlor has a restored gilt antique mirror above the carved marble fireplace. On the mantel stands a French bronze clock and majolica ginger jars. A mixture of Hepplewhite-, Chippendale-, and Queen Anne-style furniture surrounds the beautiful Serapi rug dated 1860.

The dining room is furnished with Queen Anne chairs, a Georgian table, and a Sheraton sideboard. The silver is English and Oriental vases sit on the mantel. Large dividing doors can isolate this room from the parlor. The fabric of the matching drapes in both these rooms is called Grecian Portal.

This English crystal chandelier sends sparkles of light throughout the dining room.

Morel House

117 West Perry Street

Morel House, north elevation, over-looking Orleans Square, was built in 1828.

This wide entrance hallway has some interesting pieces, in particular the English Hepplewhite linen press of satinwood inlaid with rosewood, ca. 1785, and the mahogany English clock in the background, ca. 1780.

The living room boasts a prized mahogany Chippendale secretary/bookcase, ca. 1780.

The Morel House dining room is dominated by an English sideboard with inlaid panels, ca. 1850. The painted ceiling borders are by a local artist.

Capt. L. J. Guilmartin House

110 West Harris Street

The charming dining room has a gilded English Chippendale mirror, ca. 1785. A pair of Imari urns overlook the Tiffany silver and fine Davenport china laid out for dinner guests.

The Dutch inlaid fruitwood secretary in the parlor, ca. 1870, has a Tiffany desk set.

Capt. L. J. Guilmartin House was built in 1871. Originally divided, the parlor was made into one large room during modernization.

Battersby-Hartridge House

119 East Charlton Street

The Greek Revival Battersby-Hartridge House may have been designed by John S. Norris, architect of the neighboring Andrew Low mansion. Built in 1852 for cotton merchant William Battersby, it features a striking shuttered balcony facing a walled parterre garden in the Charleston style.

The antebellum side garden was laid out in 1852 by Emmelyn Hartridge Battersby.

Battersby Hartridge House, north elevation, with double balcony facing Lafayette Square.

Battersby-Hartridge House dining room reflecting interior changes made in the 1880s by architect William G. Preston. Matching motifs on both the carpet and wallpaper add charm to this inviting room.

The shuttered porch overlooking the Battersby-Hartridge House parterre garden.

Once a double parlor, this living room is comfortably furnished. The Japanese screen still contains original household documents between the parchments. A Regency spoon-back chair on casters is in the foreground. The Irish pine dealwood breakfront houses family china, glassware, and books.

Russell House

117 East Jones Street

This brick row house, built in 1853 by Eliza Jewett for her granddaughter, was restored in the 1970s after serving as one of Savannah's first bed and breakfast inns. Now a private home, the floors and exposed brickwork are original and serve to enhance the decor.

The elevated second-floor entrance is typical of Savannah houses.

The entrance hall has many historic prints lining the wall reflecting the interests of the owner.

The parlor, overlooking Jones Street, is a showplace of antiques, paintings, and objets d'art.

Russell House dining room with bookshelf displays of historical miniatures and artifacts.

The nineteenth-century cabinet holds rare coins, medals, and miniatures relating to the Revolutionary and Civil wars.

The Confederate flag over the fireplace in the upstairs study/den is ca. 1860.

Thomas-Levy House

12 East Taylor Street

This magnificent house was built for Daniel Thomas in 1869 at a cost of $6,000 and remodelled by department store owner B. H. Levy in 1896 for an additional $3,000 in the Second Empire Baroque style.

Thomas-Levy House was fully restored by its present owners in 1976. It serves as their home with an antique map and print shop at basement level.

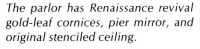

The solarium, added in 1896, is graced by a plaster-of-Paris statue by Charleston sculptor Willard Hirsh.

The parlor has Renaissance revival gold-leaf cornices, pier mirror, and original stenciled ceiling.

The stenciled ceiling in the dining room was recreated by Savannah artist Lori Sturgess.

Thomas-Levy House parlor looking toward the sunlit dining room.

The mahogany four-poster bed was made in the West Indies about 1825.

Mickve Israel Temple

20 East Gordon Street

Mickve Israel, founded by Spanish and Portuguese Jews in July 1733, is the third oldest Jewish congregation in America.

Mickve Israel Temple, overlooking Monterey Square, is the only Gothic synagogue in the United States.

Interior of the Mickve Israel Temple. The present synagogue was consecrated on April 11, 1878.

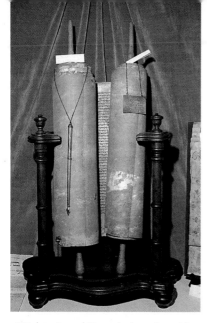

Mickve Israel Temple has the oldest Torah in America, kept in a showcase and dating from 1733.

Sheftall Cemetery is located at Garrard Street near Cohen Street.

The Old Jewish Burial Grounds, the Sheftall family cemetery gates.

Sheftall Cemetery was the first enclosed burial ground in Savannah.

The Gastonian Inn

220 East Gaston Street

The Gastonian Inn was built in 1868 in the Italianate style for Savannah grocer Aaron Champion.

The main hallway has a crystal chandelier and an old English grandfather clock on the landing.

The entrance hall to the Annex has a unique hand-carved lattice screen and seat original to the house to welcome visitors.

The Gastonian Inn parlor decorated for Christmas featuring stippled walls in Scuppernong Green, an historic Savannah color named after a Southern grape, and notable antiques like the Chippendale secretary, ca. 1780, a Sheraton-style sofa, ca. 1810, and a two-tier mahogany table, ca. 1810, illuminated by a Waterford crystal chandelier.

The luxurious Caracella Suite bedroom has a canopied king-sized Charleston Rice carved bed, Empire reclining couch, and antique Kirman rug.

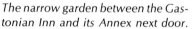

The narrow garden between the Gastonian Inn and its Annex next door.

The Caracalla Suite also has an eight-foot jacuzzi bathtub with solid brass fittings and ceiling-to-floor drapes, providing the ultimate in comfort. Since 1985 the present owners have spent nearly two million dollars restoring the Gastonian's nineteenth-century ambience.

George Baldwin House

225 East Hall Street

Architect William Gibbons Preston designed and built this Queen Anne-style mansion in 1887. The plans still sit in the Boston Public Library.

The George Baldwin House has exquisite exterior brickwork detail in terra-cotta ornamentation, typical of the Queen Anne style.

A grand central stairway, heavy carved columns, and half-panelled walls make this magnificent entrance hall the focal point of the house. The alcove reception room was said to be used for courting.

The upper stairwell has a cozy window seat and stained glass.

The parlor is furnished with family heirlooms brought here from Waynesboro, Georgia when the current owner purchased the house. Art Nouveau vases from Austria, ca. 1895, stand on the mantel, over which hangs a portrait of Julia Philips Abbot.

The hand-carved four-poster Southern bed in the George Baldwin House is from the early 1800s.

Sunlight streams into this handsome dining room with a converted gasolier, ca. 1800, from Augusta, Georgia, hanging from the painted ceiling.

Smithfield Cottage

118 West Hall Street

Smithfield Cottage was built in 1888 in the Queen Anne style by architect Alfred S. Eichberg for Jessy Parker Williams, who was a wealthy plantation owner from Statesboro, Georgia.

Dark stained oak beams distinguish the entrance hall. Chinese terracotta Foo dogs before the original fireplace are late nineteenth century.

The hand-carved mantel over the fireplace and curlicue woodwork entrance to the alcove add warmth to the parlor.

Note the Tiffany lamp, ca. 1875, that is original to the house. The beautiful glasswork in the stairway and throughout the house is recognized as the work of Mr. Lewis Comfort Tiffany.

Smithfield Cottage bedroom has a Victorian bed made in Boston, ca. 1875, of faux-grain hardwood.

The dining room with a decorative ceiling and frieze in a seashell, Georgia peach, and azalea motif. The impressive silver and glass collection is laid out for special occasions around a silver centerpiece inscribed, "Made for the Great English Silver Exposition 1888."

Smithfield Cottage library has an English country look—a fireside chair, old books and curios, and an unabridged dictionary lying open under the lamp.

Elizabeth on 37th Street Restaurant

105 East 37th Street

This Palladian-style house, north elevation, was built in 1900. New owners transformed it into the Elizabeth on 37th Street Restaurant in the early 1980s.

Looking through the lobby to the dessert room.

A table with a romantic window view of the front garden, where the owner grows herbs for culinary use.

The entrance hall and fireplace welcome guests to gourmet dining.

Elizabeth on 37th Street Restaurant serves classic Southern dishes in imaginative ways, drawing customers from coast to coast.

The dessert serving area and bar with a glass window depicting Historic Savannah.

The rear dining area.

Isle of Hope

Isaac Beckett House

9 Bluff Drive

The Isaac Beckett House, overlooking the Skidaway River, was built in 1872 for the niece of Dr. Louis Le Conte.

The parlor has special support timbers built to withstand hurricanes—the wall interiors are tongue and groove and between each piece of wood a narrow sheet of metal runs from floor to ceiling; also iron rods in the walls add support.

The dining room gas and electric chandeliers, here and in the parlor, were made by Juliette Low, founder of the Girl Scouts.

Wormsloe Plantation Historic Site

37601 Skidaway Road

Wormsloe was the fortified colonial estate of Noble Jones, who came with Oglethorpe on the ship *Anne* in 1733. Jones' family lived here over two hundred years, producing cotton, grapes, rice, indigo, and silk. From here Jones and a company of marines defended Savannah from the Spanish to the south. The tabby ruins of Jones' dwelling, built between 1739 and 1745, remain as well as the earthworks of Fort Wimberly, set up by the Confederates in 1861.

The Wormsloe Plantation Historic Site gateway was added in 1913.

The Jones family cemetery at the Wormsloe Plantation Historic Site.

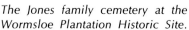

The tabby ruins of the original Jones home.

Awe-inspiring live oak trees line the drive to the house site and visitor center.

Suburbs

Bethesda Home for Boys and Chapel

9520 Ferguson Avenue

The entrance to the 500-acre campus.

The Bethesda Home for Boys was founded by Rev. George Whitefield in 1740, with the encouragement of Oglethorpe and other colonists, making it the oldest orphanage in the United States.

Many distinguished people have gotten their start in life at Bethesda, including Georgia governor John Milledge and Gen. Lachlan McIntosh.

Bethesda Chapel was built between 1916 and 1924 as a gift from the Georgia Society of Colonial Dames of America.

An uncluttered design creates a simple devotional atmosphere.

Bonaventure Cemetery

Bonaventure Road—Thunderbolt

Bonaventure Cemetery was once the plantation home of Colonel Mulryne in the 1700s.

Bonaventure Cemetery was established as a burial ground in 1847.

Towering moss-draped live oaks have stood guard over gravestones for more than a century.

Grove Point Plantation

Grove Point Road

Mystery surrounds Grove Point Plantation. The original land grant of two 500-acre tracts situated between the Ogeechee and Grove rivers dates from England's King George III in 1774. The pirate Blackbeard once used the land as a slave compound, according to legend. Romantics say that treasure remains today right where Blackbeard buried it.

Dr. Cheeves built a German-style castle here in 1830 complete with turrets. Union troops under General Sherman plundered and burned the house in 1864. Dr. Cheeves died of a heart attack on the front steps. Slaves buried the family silver— where, no one knows.

The present house was built in 1886. Rice was the principal crop, though experiments were conducted with the tea plant, a relative of the camelia. A drive down the winding shell road to Grove Point, under century-old magnolia and live oak trees draped in Spanish moss, takes one to a far-off time.

Grove Point Plantation, south elevation, stands as a reminder of a time when the land provided for many of its inhabitants' needs.

The parlor/sitting room at Grove Point is where guests at this private plantation gather of an evening to share their discoveries.

The intimate dining room at Grove Point has a floor-level window which opens onto the front porch.

This comfortably furnished guest bedroom in rich red and green over-looks a meadow of ancient live oaks.

MAP OF SAVANNAH

SAVANNAH RIVER

RIVERFRONT PLAZA

RIVER ST.

RIVER ST.

WILLIAMSON

FACTORS WALK

FACTORS WALK

Emmet Park

◄ To 17 N., 21 & Hwy. 80 W.

To 17 N. & Talmadge Bridge ►

W. BOUNDARY

FAHM

W. BROAD

W. BAY

BULL

E. BAY

E. BAY

E. BAY

80 E. (to Forts & Beaches) ►

W. BRYAN

E. BRYAN

E. BRYAN

Franklin Square

Ellis Square

W. ST. JULIAN

Johnson Square

E. ST. JULIAN

Reynolds Square

Warren Square

Washington Square

W. CONGRESS

E. CONGRESS

E. CONGRESS

COUNTY COURTHOUSE

MONTGOMERY

JEFFERSON

BARNARD

WHITAKER

W. BROUGHTON

W. BROUGHTON

E. BROUGHTON

DRAYTON

ABERCORN

LINCOLN

HABERSHAM

PRICE

HOUSTON

E. BROAD

E. BROUGHTON

E. BROUGHTON

W. STATE

W. STATE

E. STATE

E. STATE

E. STATE

Liberty Square

Telfair Square

Wright Square

W. PRESIDENT

E. PRESIDENT

Oglethorpe Square

Columbia Square

E. PRESIDENT

Greene Square

W. YORK

W. YORK

E. YORK

E. YORK

W. OGLETHORPE

W. OGLETHORPE

W. OGLETHORPE

E. OGLETHORPE

E. OGLETHORPE

E. OGLETHORPE

TURNER

Elbert Square

Orleans Square

W. HULL

E. HULL

E. HULL

COLONIAL PARK CEMETERY

E. McDONOUGH

Crawford Square

W. McDONOUGH

Chippewa Square

E. McDONOUGH

W. PERRY

E. PERRY

E. PERRY

LOUISVILLE

TATTNALL

W. LIBERTY

E. LIBERTY

E. LIBERTY

W. HARRIS

E. HARRIS

E. HARRIS

Pulaski Square

Madison Square

E. MACON

Lafayette Square

Troup Square

E. MACON

W. CHARLTON

E. CHARLTON

E. CHARLTON

W. JONES

E. JONES

E. JONES

BERRIEN

W. TAYLOR

E. TAYLOR

E. TAYLOR

To Mun. Airport

Chatham Square

W. WAYNE

Monterey Square

E. WAYNE

Calhoun Square

Whitefield Square

16 West

16 East

W. BROAD

MONTGOMERY

ALICE

JEFFERSON

TATTNALL

BARNARD

W. GORDON

E. GORDON

BULL

DRAYTON

ABERCORN

LINCOLN

E. GORDON

HABERSHAM

PRICE

E. GORDON

N

S

To 17 S. & Hwy. 80

W. GASTON

E. GASTON

E. GASTON

W. HUNTINGDON

E. HUNTINGDON

E. HUNTINGDON

FORSYTH PARK

W. HALL

E. HALL

VICTORIAN DISTRICT